The Life and Work of...

Joseph Turner

Jayne Woodhouse

Heinemann
LIBRARY

H www.heinemann.co.uk
Visit our website to find out more information about Heinemann Library books.

To order:
☎ Phone 44 (0) 1865 888066
📄 Send a fax to 44 (0) 1865 314091
💻 Visit the Heinemann Bookshop at www.heinemann.co.uk to browse our catalogue and order online.

First published in Great Britain by Heinemann Library,
Halley Court, Jordan Hill, Oxford OX2 8EJ
a division of Reed Educational and Professional
Publishing Ltd.
Heinemann is a registered trademark of Reed
Educational & Professional Publishing Ltd.

OXFORD MELBOURNE AUCKLAND
JOHANNESBURG BLANTYRE GABORONE
IBADAN PORTSMOUTH (NH) USA CHICAGO

Designed by Celia Floyd
Illustrations by Sally Barton
Originated by Dot Gradations
Printed in Hong Kong/China

04 03 02 01 00
10 9 8 7 6 5 4 3 2 1
ISBN 0 431 09197 8

British Library Cataloguing in Publication Data

Woodhouse, Jayne
Life and work of Joseph Turner
1. Turner, J. M. W. (Joseph Mallord William), 1775-
1851 – Juvenile literature
2. Painters – Great Britain – Biography – Juvenile
literature
3. Painting, Modern, 19th century – Great Britain –
Juvenile literature
4. Painting, British – Juvenile literature
I. Title II. Joseph Turner
759.2

Acknowledgements
The Publishers would like to thank the following for
permission to reproduce photographs:

Ashmolean Museum, Oxford: p7; Bridgeman Art Library:
National Gallery, London pp5, 9, Reading University,
Berkshire p24, Agnew & Sons, London p27; E T Archive:
p4; Indianapolis Museum of Art, gift in memory of Dr
and Mrs Hugo O Pantzer: p11; Robert Harding Picture
Library: Ellen Rooney pp18, 20, 26, 28; Tate Picture
Library: pp19, 21, 23, 25, 29; The Whitworth Art Gallery:
p15; Yale Center for British Art: Paul Mellon Collection
p12

Cover photograph reproduced with permission of The
Bridgeman Art Library

Every effort has been made to contact copyright holders
of any material reproduced in this book. Any omissions
will be rectified in subsequent printings if notice is given
to the Publisher.

Any words appearing in the text in bold, **like this**, are
explained in the Glossary.

Contents

Who was Joseph Turner?

Joseph Mallord William Turner is one of the greatest English artists. His work changed the way people thought about **landscape** painting.

Joseph is often called 'the painter of light'.
This is because of the special way he showed the
changing sky and weather in his paintings.

Early years

Joseph was born in this house in London, on 23 April 1775, just over 200 years ago. His father was a barber. His mother was unwell for much of her life.

Joseph started drawing when he was just a boy. His father was very proud of his pictures and hung them in his shop. Joseph drew this picture when he was 12 years old.

A love of the sea

When he was young, Joseph loved to watch the ships on the River Thames in London. One day he saw a picture of a ship at sea. This made him decide to be a painter.

8

All his life Joseph painted ships and the sea. In 1838, when he was 63, he painted this picture of a famous fighting ship on its last journey.

Learning to be an artist

When he was 14, Joseph went to the **Royal Academy** in London to study art. His first tasks were to draw **statues** from ancient Greece and Rome.

A year later, in 1790, Joseph **exhibited** his first painting at the Royal Academy. He was only 15 years old, but it was already clear that he was very talented.

The Royal Academy

Joseph **exhibited** his paintings at the **Royal Academy** for the rest of his life. This picture shows people visiting the **gallery** in Joseph's time. Look how close together the paintings are.

Joseph became a **professor** at the Royal Academy when he was 32. He made many careful drawings, like this one, to teach other artists about painting and drawing.

Travels in Britain

From the age of 17, Joseph began the first of his many travels. He was always looking for something new to draw and paint.

At first Joseph visited places in Britain. His first paintings were **watercolours** of the things he saw. Joseph painted Canterbury **Cathedral** in 1794, when he was 19.

Travels in Europe

In his lifetime, Joseph travelled to many places all over Europe. Travelling was much slower and harder then. There were no cars or aeroplanes. Joseph often walked 15 kilometres in a day.

Joseph made **sketches** of what he saw. Later he would turn his sketches into finished paintings. He painted this scene of the German countryside when he was 45, three years after his visit there.

Old Masters

In 1802, when he was 27, Joseph visited the Louvre Museum in Paris, France. He studied the Louvre's famous collection of **Old Masters**. This is a photograph of the Louvre today.

Joseph liked the Old Masters. He started to paint with **oils** like they did. This oil painting is in the same **style** as Poussin, a great French painter from the 17th century.

A visitor at Petworth

One man who really liked Joseph's work was Lord Egremont. He was the owner of Petworth, a great country house. Egremont collected many of Joseph's pictures. This is Petworth House today.

From the age of 34, Joseph often visited
Petworth. He had his own **studio** there. He
made many **sketches** and paintings of the
house and its huge grounds.

Sketches

Joseph liked to paint things he had seen himself. In 1810 he was staying in Yorkshire, in the north of England. A terrible storm came up and Joseph quickly made **sketches** of it on the back of a letter.

He used those sketches to help him make this painting two years later. You can see the storm sweeping across the mountains.

Ways of working

Joseph often worked in unusual ways. Sometimes he finished his pictures while they hung on the **gallery** walls, the day before the **exhibition** opened!

This painting shows a ship caught in a snow storm. Joseph said that he was on this ship that day. He asked the sailors to tie him to the mast so he could see what the storm was really like.

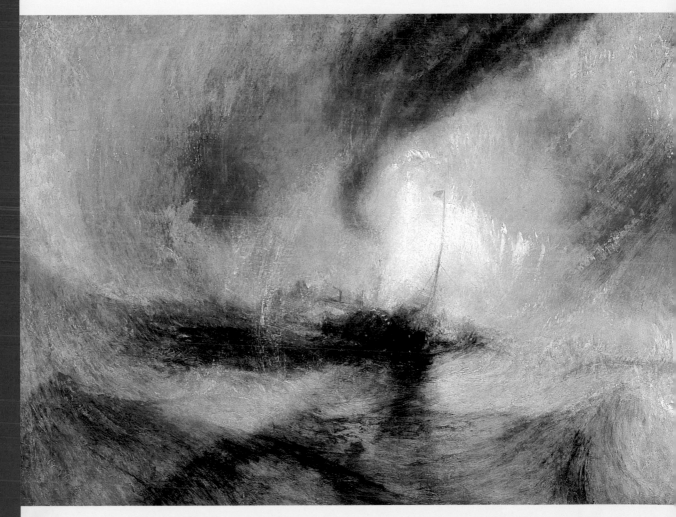

New directions

An important change in Joseph's work came on his first visit to Venice, Italy, in 1819. The dazzling Italian light gave him new ideas about how to show shape and colour.

Joseph returned to Venice several times. He painted many pictures of its famous buildings and waterways. He finished this one in 1840, when he was 65.

Joseph dies

Joseph continued to paint almost to the end of his life. He died in 1851, aged 76. He was buried in St Paul's **Cathedral**, London. In his will, Joseph left many of his paintings to the British people.

Joseph's later paintings were more **abstract**. They were full of swirling colours of light. At the time people didn't like these paintings. They called them 'pictures of nothing'. Now people think they are Turner's **masterpieces**.

Timeline

1775	Joseph Turner born in London on 23 April.
1789	Joseph starts studying art at the **Royal Academy**.
1790	Joseph's first painting is **exhibited**.
1792	Joseph goes on his first **sketching** tour in England and Wales.
1802	Joseph goes on his first tour abroad visiting France and Switzerland.
1804	Joseph opens his own **gallery**.
1807	Joseph becomes a **professor** at the Royal Academy.
1809	Joseph makes his first visit to Petworth House.
1819	Joseph's first visit to Venice, Italy.
1828, 1833, 1840	Joseph revisits Italy several times.
1837	Victoria becomes Queen of England.
1837	Lord Egremont dies.
1840	The artist Claude Monet is born in France.
1850	Joseph has his last exhibition at Royal Academy.
1851	Joseph dies on 19 December.
1853	The artist Vincent van Gogh is born in Holland.
1879	The artist Paul Klee is born in Switzerland.
1897	Joseph's works go on display at the new National Gallery of British Art (now called the Tate Gallery) in London.
1987	A special gallery (the Clore Gallery) is opened at the Tate Gallery to show Joseph's works.

Glossary

abstract   art which suggests feelings and thoughts instead of looking like objects, people or places

cathedral   large and important church

exhibit   to show and sell works of art in public

exhibition   show and sale of works of art in public

gallery   room or building where works of art are shown

landscape   painting or drawing of the countryside

masterpiece   great work of art

oils   type of paint mixed with oil

Old Masters   famous artists from earlier times

professor   person who teaches at university or college

Royal Academy   training school for artists, and place where works of art are exhibited

sketch   unfinished drawing or painting

statue   carved, moulded or sculptured figures

studio   special room or building where an artist works

style   particular way an artist does his/her work

watercolour   type of paint mixed with water

More books to read

Changing Colour, Looking at pictures, Joy Richardson, Franklin Watts

Famous Lives: Artists, J Powell, Wayland.

Looking at pictures, A& C Black

You can also visit the Tate Gallery web site on: www.tate.org.uk

More paintings to see

Many of Joseph Turner's famous paintings can be seen in the Clore Gallery at the Tate Gallery, London.

Buttermere Lake, Joseph Turner, Tate Gallery, London

The Farnley Book of Birds, Joseph Turner, Leeds Museums and Galleries, Leeds

Ship and Cutter, Joseph Turner, Fitzwilliam Museum, Cambridge

Index